I Had a
Replacement, Now
What?

(What to Expect After Knee Replacement Surgery)

Kimberly Dixon, M.Ed., CPC, CCRC

Contributions by:

Dr. Krishana Clark, B.S., C-PT, D.C.

&

Dr. Christopher Girdis, B.S., D.C.

ISBN: 1535280913
ISBN-13: 9781535280914

DEDICATION

I dedicate this book to my surgeon Dr. Michael Comstock, M.D. Thank you for listening to my story and replacing my knees. Thank you for giving me my life back! Words cannot express how grateful I am for you. Your medical knowledge and skill make you a gifted surgeon. Your heart and compassion towards people make you a great man. Thank you.

CONTENTS

ACKNOWLEDGMENTS

Thank you to my parents, Sharon Simmons and Samuel Dixon, for your love and support.

A special thank you to my best friend Kesha for caring for me after both knee replacements. Having you by my side made everything better.

Thank you to my family and friends that prepared meals, cleaned house, cared for my cats and made sure all my needs were met. Thank you Mama, Val, Tammy, Odessa, Courtney and Vanessa. You guys are the best!

Lastly and most importantly, I want to thank God for teaching me how to trust, how to remain hopeful, and how to persevere. To God be the glory!

PREFACE

I Had a Knee Replacement, Now What?, is the last book in the Now What book series on arthritis and knee replacement surgery. But it is not the end of the story. Your story continues long after you physically heal from surgery. You have the power to re-write your story so that it continues in the manner in which you choose. I pray that these books provided you with some insight, inspiration and motivation to charge forward, to seize the day and to build the life you desire with your new artificial knee(s).

I wrote these books to empower you and dispel some of the myths and misinformation about arthritis and knee replacement. I was fortunate to always have great surgeons and physical therapists, but there is a lot of information that falls between the cracks between the surgeon, physical therapist and insurance company. These books attempt to fill in the gap while sharing some of my experiences. They aren't an all-inclusive guide because every patient is different. They have different medical conditions and different experiences.

I intentionally made all three books short. They are a quick, easy read. The weeks prior to surgery and afterwards are busy. There are pre-operative appointments, home to-do lists and other arrangements to be made. After surgery, there are post-operative visits and lots of physical therapy appointments. At this time in your life, many don't have the time or the inclination to read a 200 page guide. The books are written in simple language and get straight to the point for that reason.

However, I encourage you to complete the exercises included in the books. They are designed to prompt you to think about the decisions you make consciously and unconsciously that impact your recovery and your life. These questions though quite simple help you make decisions that empower, encourage, inspire and motivate you.

It brought me great joy to write this series. My greatest desire is to help people in pain. That is the purpose for my life. It is my mission. Thank you for allowing me to share part of my story with you.

Be blessed and remember to always, live joyfully.

Kimberly

INTRODUCTION

3Not only this, but we also rejoice in our sufferings, knowing that suffering produces perseverance; 4and perseverance, proven character; and proven character, hope: 5and hope doesn't disappoint us, because God's love has been poured out into our hearts through the Holy Spirit who was given to us.
- Romans 5:3-5

My Background

No one ever thought they would see this day. The day when I have two perfectly straight legs.

A surge of emotion shot through my body like a lightning bolt when I saw my Dad's face. His eyes lit up with amazement, his smile was as wide as the ocean as I walked through his front door. No leg brace, no cane, no bowed legs. I said fighting back my own tears, "Look Daddy, I have two new knees." April 18, 2016 was the first time my 73 year old father saw me with straight legs.

My mother, sister, brother, aunts and uncles all had the same reaction. Some cried, some stared in quiet disbelief and some turned their face away to hide the flood of emotion. I knew exactly what they felt seeing me for the first time. It was the same way I felt.

Every time I look down and see two straight legs I smile. Every time I walk with no pain I smile. For months after surgery I had occasions when silent tears of joy rolled down my face. I always knew that my knees would be replaced someday. I waited so long because of my young age, that when my knees were finally replaced it didn't seem real.

I was bow-legged from birth to 44 years old. For the first time in my life when I look down, I see straight legs. This still doesn't seem real to me at times. It definitely doesn't look real when I see my image in a mirror. I was bow-legged. I would always be bow-legged or so I thought.

Having straight legs brought so many changes. The most drastic and the most unbelievable is that I no longer suffer with chronic arthritis pain. There was a point when I thought my pain would never end. I was fearful I would die in this deep, dark pit. Arthritis is by no means terminal. The pain, sadness, darkness and heartbreak it causes can be.

I kept trusting God while in my valley, I remained hopeful that my pain would end, and that I would use my life as an instrument to help others. That day has come.

When I became a life coach, I told my sister that I wanted my life to be unrecognizable from one year to the next. When I made that statement, I spoke in reference to becoming more open-minded and more open to the possibilities available to me. I didn't realize when I made that statement that in less than two years I would become physically unrecognizable. In the past people recognized me because of my walk, feet turned inward, hips swaying and wide bowed legs. Today my feet no longer turn inward, my legs are perfectly straight and I am actually an inch taller (In my teens I was 5'9. As the space in my joints decreased and my legs bowed more, I shrunk to 5'8).

Today I am 5'9 again. And truly unrecognizable!

The little girl in the red dress is me, circa 1973.

Kimberly Dixon, M.Ed., CPC, CCRC

What Happens in a Knee Replacement

Knee replacement surgery is exactly as it sounds. The surgery involves removing the damaged natural joint and replacing it with artificial parts referred to as implants or prostheses.

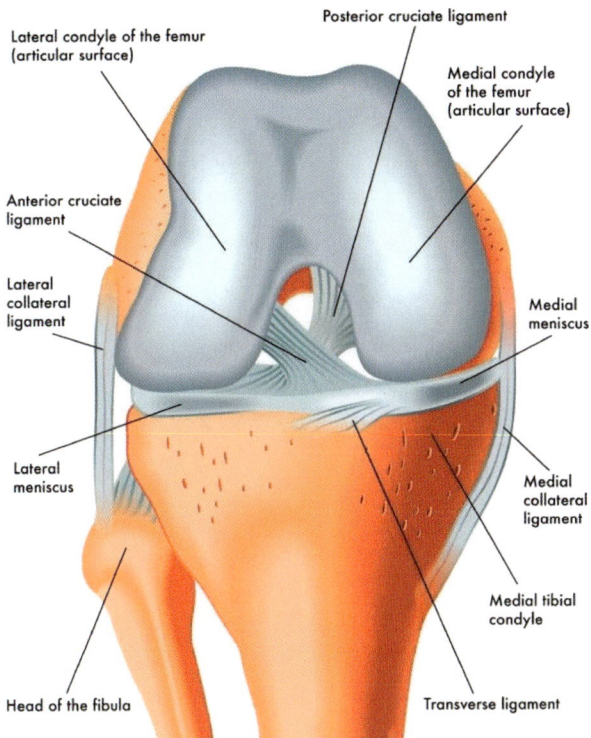

Normal Knee anatomy

Knee replacement becomes necessary when the knee joint is damaged as a result of arthritis, an injury, or wear and tear which refers to the natural changes that occur as a result of aging and normal use. These may cause bone spurs, cartilage damage or ligament tears. Once the severity of cartilage loss reaches the point in which there is exposed bone, a knee replacement becomes necessary. Exposed bone causes bone to rub against bone instead the cushioning cartilage creates.

STAGE OF KNEE OSTEOARTHRITIS

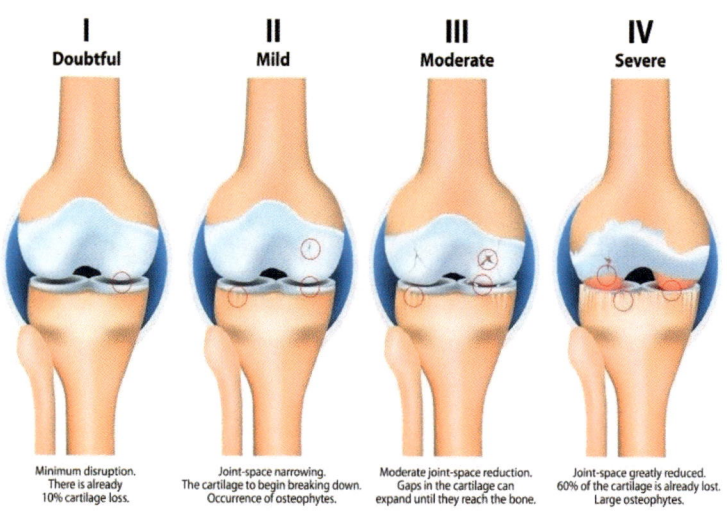

I	II	III	IV
Doubtful	Mild	Moderate	Severe
Minimum disruption. There is already 10% cartilage loss.	Joint-space narrowing. The cartilage to begin breaking down. Occurrence of osteophytes.	Moderate joint-space reduction. Gaps in the cartilage can expand until they reach the bone.	Joint-space greatly reduced. 60% of the cartilage is already lost. Large osteophytes.

During the total knee replacement surgery (TKR), the damaged ends of the femur (thigh bone) and tibia (shin bone) are removed, and the bone is shaped to secure the prosthesis. A spacer sits between the artificial parts attached to the femur and the tibia.

Total Knee Replacement

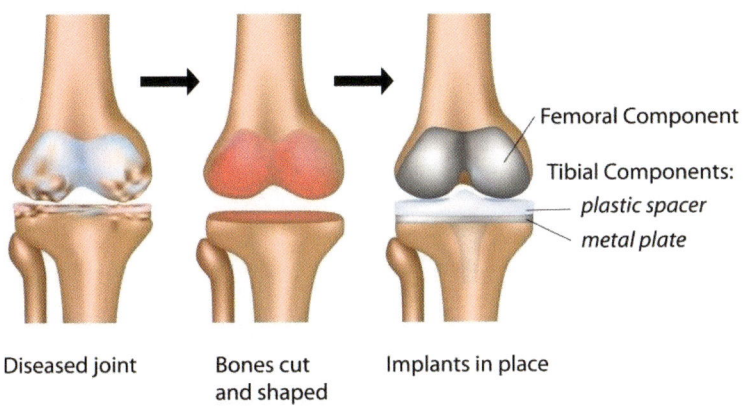

Femoral Component

Tibial Components:
plastic spacer
metal plate

Diseased joint | Bones cut and shaped | Implants in place

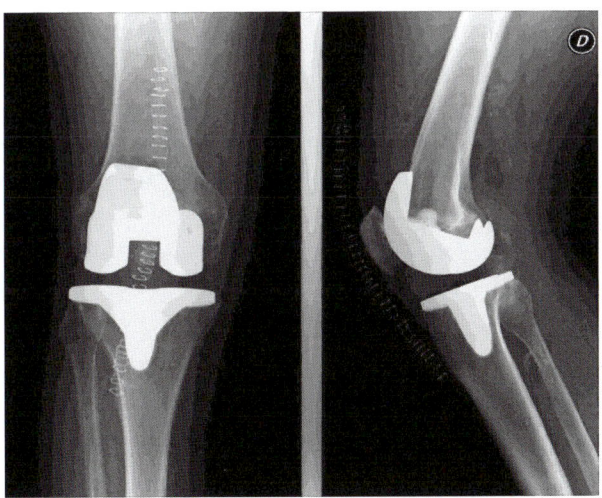

X-ray of a knee with total knee replacement prosthesis.

There are instances when a partial knee replacement is a viable option. If damage is localized to one side of the knee, then a partial replacement may be recommended. The undamaged portion of the knee is left intact. However, the patient must have an intact, functioning anterior cruciate ligament (ACL) to get a partial knee replacement.

In 2010, I had ACL reconstruction surgery for that very reason. At the time the arthritis in my right knee was compartmentalized to the inner portion of my knee, but my ACL was a mangled mess. I underwent ACL reconstruction so that I qualified for a partial knee replacement.

I don't waste my time with regrets or ruminating over the past but if there is one surgery I would opt not to do if I could go back in time, it would be the ACL reconstruction surgery. The pain after that surgery was brutal. It was much worse than the pain from total knee replacement.

I went through months of physical therapy only to discover nine months later that the arthritis spread to under my kneecap and the other side of my knee. I no longer qualified for a partial knee replacement. Some surgeons and physical therapists don't like partials for that very reason. Arthritis is progressive and often spreads. Someone that opts for a partial replacement may eventually still need a total knee. With that being said, every situation is different. You and your surgeon need to weigh all the options and make the best decision for you based on your medical history and needs.

The ACL reconstruction surgery did eventually decrease my day-to-day pain from the ACL tears but I still had arthritis which seemingly got worse every day. Within nine months of the ACL surgery I wore a leg brace. I wore that leg brace for the next four years.

An orthopedic surgeon performs total knee replacement. An assistant surgeon and anesthesiologist are present during the surgery along with surgical technicians and nurses. Other personnel may be present. The surgeon may use a robotic arm during the surgery, as well.

Anesthesia is administered for every surgery to decrease pain and keep the patient comfortable during and after surgery. An anesthesiologist administers anesthesia and monitors the patient. The type of anesthesia used depends on the surgery type, surgery site, and the complexity of the surgery.

Anesthesia types include: local, regional or general.

Local anesthesia is used for small sites and the patient is awake.

Regional anesthesia numbs part of the body and is common with arm and leg surgeries, but can be used for other surgeries as well. Two common types of regional anesthesia are an epidural (used in childbirth) and spinal (common in orthopedic surgeries).

General anesthesia makes the patient fully unconscious and may involve the insertion of a breathing tube. If you have a scratchy throat after surgery, it is probably because of a breathing tube.

Anesthesia types are often combined to achieve the best results. For instance, for my total right knee, I had general anesthesia and a nerve block. For my left knee, I had spinal anesthesia and a nerve block.

I prefer regional anesthesia, because after surgery I am much more alert and I don't experience the nausea that general anesthesia sometimes causes. The anesthesia nurse will typically discuss the type of anesthesia planned and answer any questions you have concerning anesthesia during your pre-operative visit. This visit occurs 1-14 days prior to surgery.

I always schedule my pre-operative visit two weeks prior to surgery. This small window gives me time to address any minor issues that present themselves at the pre-operative visit. For example in 2011, I underwent gastric sleeve surgery to lose weight to reduce the pressure on my knees. My blood work showed that my potassium level was low. The doctor wrote a prescription for me to take potassium for two weeks. By my surgery date, my levels were normal. I am not sure what issues cause a surgery to get cancelled, but I would hate to arrive for surgery and have the it postponed for any reason.

The day of surgery the surgeon and anesthesiologist visit you in the pre-operative area to go over the surgery again, mark the surgery site, and answer any last minute questions.

Be sure to bring your medication list, insurance information along with any required deductibles, coinsurance or co-pays, a family member or friend as you can't undergo surgery if you arrive alone, personal effects such as eyeglasses or medical devices, and your sense of humor.

Surgery is physically and mentally taxing. Laughing, smiling and being friendly make the experience easier for you and those caring for you.

*Every surgery carries risks and/or the possibility of complications. Complications from total knee replacement may include blood clots or infection. Blood clots occur because the body's response to bleeding is to attempt to stop it by clotting. The risk of blood clots is minimized by blood thinner medication prescribed after surgery and techniques to encourage blood circulation. Reduce the risk of infection by keeping the incision clean and dry and by wearing gloves when changing dressings.

**This is a very high overview of knee replacement surgery. I am NOT a medical professional. As such, I am not offering medical advice. This book provides information from a patient's perspective, and attempts to make scientific medical information more easily understandable. As such it is not an all-inclusive manual. It is a general guide that shares information to help patients feel less anxious and apprehensive about their procedure. I gained this knowledge through my surgical history and years of asking questions.

The information presented here is strictly for informational purposes only!

**All medical decisions should be made between you and your physician based on your individual medical condition and needs.

Kimberly Dixon, M.Ed., CPC, CCRC

CHAPTER ONE
CHOICES

Life is not a continuum of pleasant choices, but of inevitable problems that call for strength, determination, and hard work.
-Indian Proverb

Congratulations, you did it! You made the choice to have knee replacement surgery!

You are now entering the next phase of your journey. During this phase you have more choices to make. The choices you make determine your outcome. Those decisions determine how much function you regain, how much of your life you get back, and what new experiences you create.

If you read the other books in the *Now What?* Series, you probably noticed that Chapter One is always about choices. Our ability to choose, to make a decision, is one of our greatest assets. When we make choices and take accountability for our choices, we hold the key to our own happiness and success.

After TKR you have the choice to do EVERYTHING required to regain full function (or as close to full function as possible) or do just enough to get by. Doing just enough to get by means you only do physical therapy when you are at a PT appointment. It means walking occasionally and not every day like you need to do. Getting by means you did just enough to say you did it (whatever the activity is), without putting forth your best effort.

Are you willing to do EVERYTHING possible to regain function or are you just going to get by?

Record your answer:

_____

_____

_____

_____

_____

It seems absurd that anyone wouldn't want to regain function or that anyone would choose just to get by. However, when you don't put forth the effort required for full recovery, that is what you are choosing. Whether the decision is made consciously or subconsciously, the choice is yours to make.

You always have a choice. Remember, the result you end with is a direct result of the decisions you make now.

Make a decision to choose you, choose your life, choose your recovery. Make a decision that benefits you long-term. Doing so requires you go through difficult times now, but the long-term result is definitely worth it.

After you make your choice, decide how you feel about it. Making the choice to do whatever is necessary to regain functionality is great. However, if you harbor negative feelings (resentment) about the decision or what the decision requires you to do, then it has a negative impact. Have positive feelings about the choice you made, to get the most benefit from it. Being positive about your choice helps get you through the tough days ahead.

Being positive simply means you focus on the positive.

So how do you focus on the positive when you are in pain, tired and cranky? You stay positive by performing positive acts.

Say thank-you for something every day.

Appreciate the ordinary. Appreciate waking up each day.

Appreciate waking up with no pain. Appreciate the walker that allows you to walk. Appreciate the cane that allows you to walk, and finally appreciate being able to walk with no assistance.

When you have arthritis, waking up in pain is common. Not being able to sleep because of pain is common. Appreciate having relief from arthritis. Showing appreciation increases the value of your new artificial knee(s) to you. There is pain after surgery, but it is a different type pain. The added benefit is that every week the surgery pain decreases!

Show appreciation to people around you. Show appreciation to your family and friends that assist and visit you after surgery. Show appreciation to the doctors, nurses and physical therapists you encounter in the hospital, and during your recovery. Showing appreciation increases gratitude.

Write in a gratitude journal. Take note of things throughout the day and write five things down every night you are grateful for, including "big" and "small" things. While recovering, regularly read your gratitude journal.

Gratitude increases positive feelings. Positive feelings release endorphins in the brain. Endorphins are the body's natural "feel good" chemicals. "Feel good" chemicals decrease pain.

Make the choice to feel positive about your decision to do everything necessary to regain function.

What do you appreciate about your life? How do you express your appreciation?

_____

_____

_____

_____

_____

What additional acts can you incorporate in your life to express and show your appreciation?

_____

_____

_____

_____

_____

Your mindset plays a major role in your outcome. Positive thoughts bring positive results. Recovering from knee replacement surgery is challenging. Maintaining a positive attitude goes a long way toward regaining the life you desire. A positive attitude reduces the stress that is an inevitable part of the healing process.

Surgery places stress on the body, mind and spirit. The actual surgery is stressful for the body. Skin, muscle and bone are cut during surgery. This causes an immediate reaction from the body. The surgery ultimately improves your quality of life and reduces your physical pain, but surgery is traumatic to the body. That trauma is stressful. The temporary reduction in mobility causes frustration, anger and sometimes sadness, which has an effect on your mental and spiritual well-being. A positive outlook and attitude help maintain clarity and a sense of purpose. The more positive your thoughts about the entire process, the less stressful the process is to your body and mind.

Negative thoughts breed more negative thoughts. Negative thinking is a vicious cycle. One negative thought leads to another negative thought which leads to another negative thought. Before you realize what happened, you play out an entire scenario in your head with nothing but negativity.

Understand that your outcome is 80% psychology and 20% mechanics. Everything we do, say and feel, originates in the mind. What you think matters.

Doing everything necessary to regain function is a choice. Staying positive is a choice. The choices you make now impact your outcome.

What will your outcome be?

_____

_____

_____

_____

_____

Are you willing to be positive about the recovery process?

_____

_____

_____

_____

_____

Tony Robbins says, "Decisions equal destiny." The decisions and choices you make today hold the key to your destiny.

CHAPTER TWO
WHAT TO EXPECT AFTER SURGERY

For I know the thoughts that I think toward you, says Yahweh,
thoughts of peace and not of evil, to give you hope in your latter end.
- Jeremiah 29:11

After knee replacement surgery, patients experience a myriad of events in different stages of recovery. This chapter helps familiarize you with some of the things you may encounter. Every patient is different, so you may experience some, all, or even quite possibly none of these events. However, as a general guideline, most patients can expect to experience these events.

As I previously stated, I am not a medical professional. You are your own best advocate. As such, it is your responsibly to follow your physician's guidelines, ask questions and seek medical attention, if you need it. The information here is not medical advice and should not be taken as such. Please contact your doctor with questions or concerns about your recovery.

When you wake up from your surgery, you are in the recovery room. You spend 1-2 hours in recovery. The goal while in recovery is to make sure your pain is controlled and that the anesthesia is wearing off as it should. There is a nurse assigned to you in recovery. They monitor your vitals closely and make you as comfortable as possible. At this time, you may get water or ice for your dry mouth, and warm blankets. Warm blankets are the best! Nothing beats that cozy, snuggly warmth.

You will likely still have electrodes attached that were used to monitor you during surgery. However, the electrodes are removed prior to going to your room.

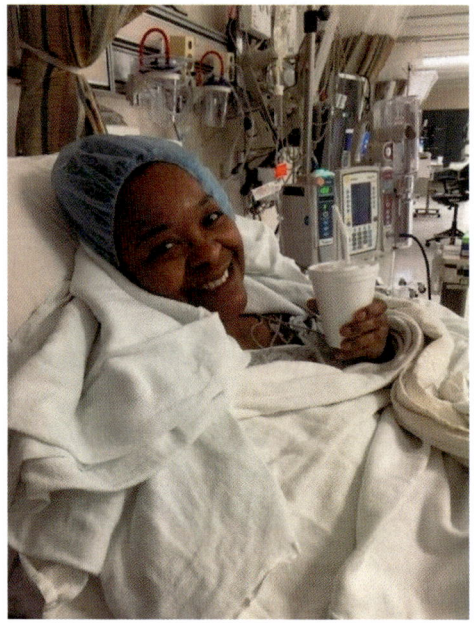

In recovery after right total knee replacement, covered in warm blankets (March 24, 2015).

As a general basis, the hospital stay after surgery is typically 1-3 days. TKR can be done outpatient but in my experiences both personally and professionally, I have not encountered anyone that had TKR as an outpatient procedure.

Both of my TKRs were performed on a Tuesday morning. With my right knee, I was hospitalized two days. I went home on Thursday. With my left knee, I was hospitalized one day. I went home on Wednesday.

After surgery, you do experience some pain. Joint replacement requires major anatomy changes. Therefore, it is traumatic to the body. Pain and swelling are a natural response to trauma. It is impossible to determine how much pain each individual will experience. Pain is perceived differently by different people.

When you wake up from surgery, you will already have a Patient-Controlled Analgesia (PCA) pump in place. I simply refer to them as a pain pump. The pain pump allows you to self-administer pain medication when you need it. The machine is programmed to deliver a specific dosage at specific intervals. It means that even if you keep pushing the button, no medication is delivered until after a specific amount of time elapses. This safety mechanism prevents overdosing.

In addition to the PCA, you will likely have compression pumps on your legs or feet. The pumps are attached to both legs/feet. The pump is like a blood pressure cuff in that it gently squeezes the legs or feet and then deflates. This action is repeated continuously while the pump is attached. Compression pumps are often used after surgery to encourage blood circulation and prevent blood clots. Compression stockings have the same purpose. Your surgeon decides which is best suited for you.

A surgical drain is already in place when you wake up in recovery. You will likely not even realize that it is there. Typically it is located just above the knee on either side of the thigh. The tube is simply there to drain excess fluids out of the surgery site. The tube is removed the day after surgery and is completely painless (the tube and the removal).

My drain tube after both surgeries was removed at the first dressing change the next day. During that first nurses visit in the morning, the bandages were changed, the catheter was removed and the drain tube removed.

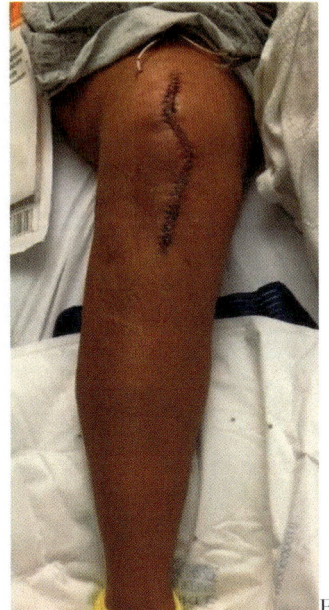

First bandage change March 25, 2015. Note the drain tube is still in place. The blue material is the Polar Care pad.

Oh, I can't forget to mention the catheter. You will have a catheter in place, as well. It is much like the drain tube in that you won't realize you have it. Sometimes the catheter is removed immediately after the surgery. It just depends on whether or not the hospital/surgeon feels it is safe for you to attempt going to the bathroom right after surgery.

The Polar Care is yet another piece of equipment that is already attached when you wake up from surgery. It circulates cold water around the surgery site to help with pain and swelling. It serves the same purpose as ice packs. It is a small cube that is filled with ice and water. The cold water circulates through tubing and a pad that is attached to your leg. You continue to use the polar care when you are released from the hospital. In the early stages of recovery you use it quite frequently especially after a PT session. As the weeks progress, you need it less.

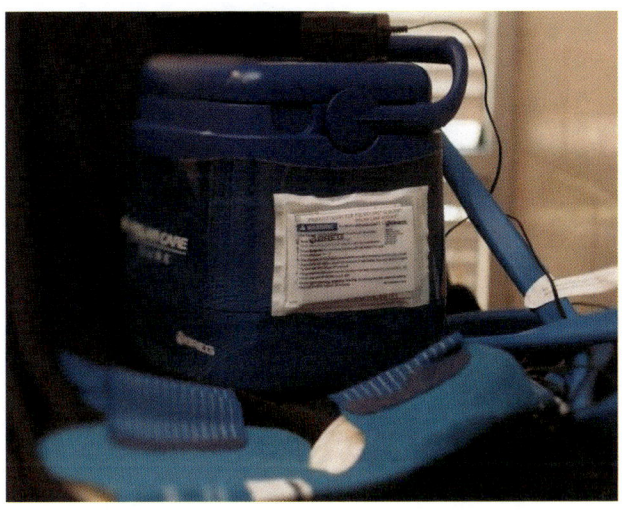

Physical therapy (PT) starts immediately. PT is such a large part of recovery, an entire chapter is dedicated to it. (CHAPTER THREE).

After a few days, bruises start to appear on and around the surgery site. The degree of bruising depends on many factors, such as the difficulty of your surgery, and whether or not a robotic arm was used.

My right leg originally had some bruising, but not an unusual amount. However, exactly two weeks after my TKR surgery I had a second surgery to revise my incision. My incision stopped healing and as a precaution the incision was opened again and cleaned. This was performed as an outpatient procedure. Due to two surgeries in the same site within two weeks, my knee and leg bruised really badly. The skin was discolored and peeled a lot. It looked quite reptilian. However the bruising, peeling and discoloration eventually subsided.

My left leg barely bruised at all. I kept waiting for the bruising to get worse, but it didn't.

27

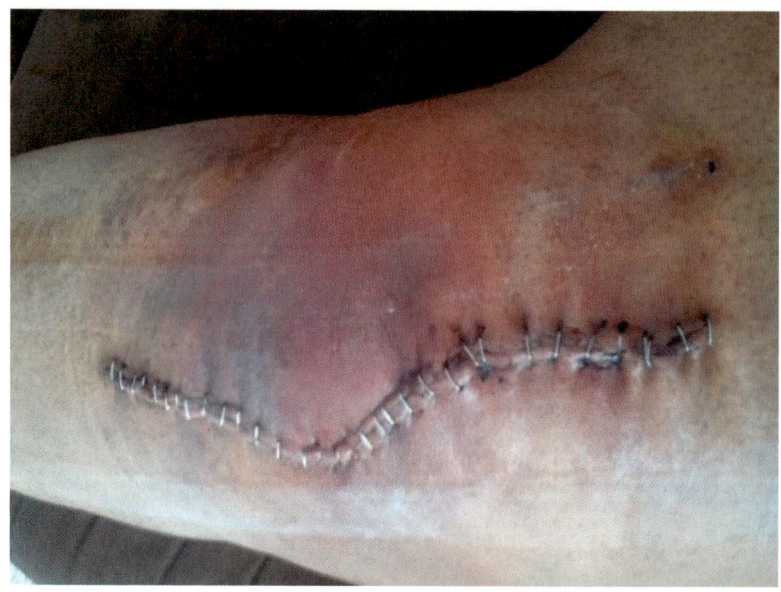

The bruising with my right knee replacement was extensive. The bruises began to appear almost immediately. This photo is six days after TKR. The bruising deepened after I had incision revision surgery two weeks after TKR. The lightning bolt shape of the incision was intentional. I had many previous surgery scars that needed to be incorporated into the new surgery site.

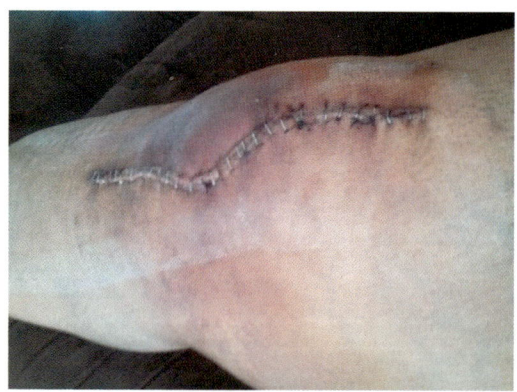

Six days after right knee TKR

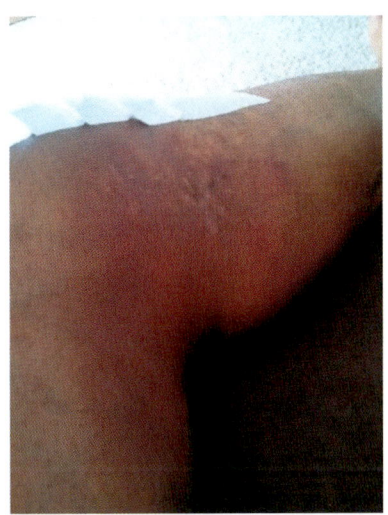

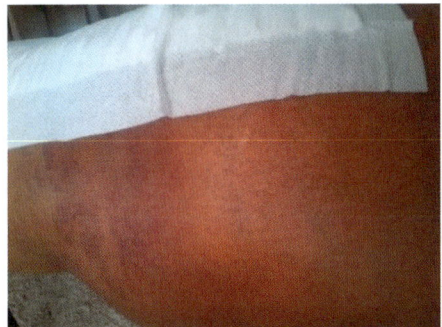

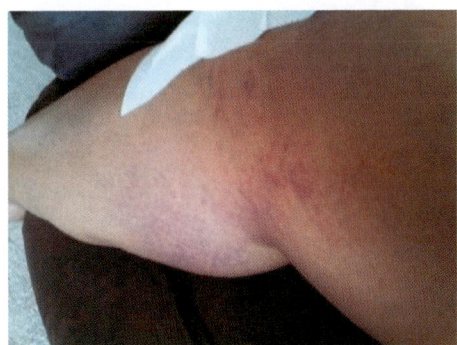

Nine days after right knee TKR

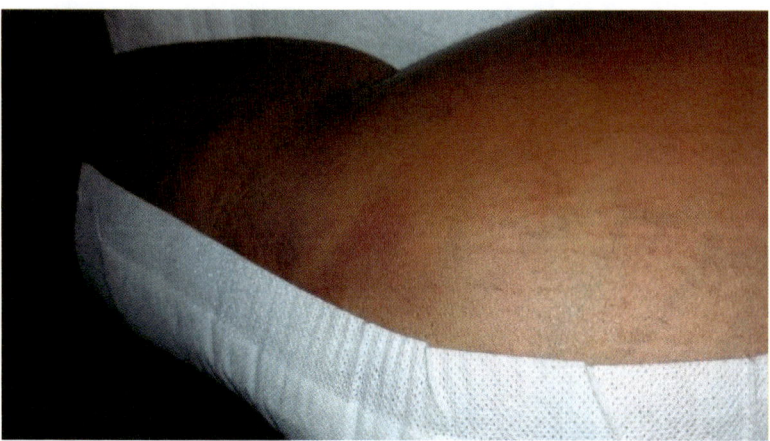

There was barely any bruising after left TKR. four days after surgery. Bruises did not develop beyond this stage.

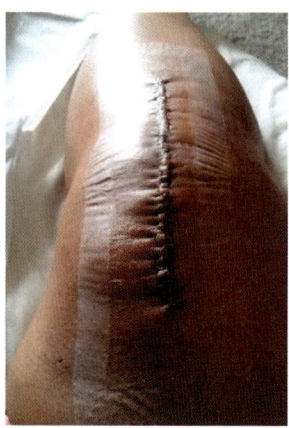

Left knee TKR incision

IV site sensitivity or soreness develops as well. It may occur while the IV is in place, but sometimes doesn't occur until after it is removed. However, IV site soreness doesn't last long, and it normally isn't severe.

Expect to use a walker right after surgery and for the first couple of weeks. Eventually you progress to a cane, but you need a walker for the first few weeks.

Using a walker feels awkward initially, but you get accustomed to it quickly. It is essential to clear a path throughout your home to accommodate the walker. Clear the path before your surgery, so when you return home, it is already done.

Upon leaving the hospital after my right TRK, the occupational nurse informed my best friend to clear the path as soon as we got home. I sat in the car for what seemed like forever, while she created a clear path from the front door to my bedroom.

Slide furniture (chairs, desk, and tables) that juts out into walking space, up to the wall. You do not recognize the small directional changes you regularly make while walking, but you recognize every directional change with a walker. When you drive a car, you make a 180 degree direction change by making a 3 point road turn. With a walker, it takes a 112 point road turn. Ok, so that is a little exaggeration. However when you first start using a walker it is an adjustment, so making a clear, straight path is very important.

It is also imperative to remove ALL area and throw rugs (including the front door mat and bathroom mats). They are a major trip hazard. Again rugs are one of those things you do not notice but get your walker hung on a rug, and you will take a nasty tumble. Save yourself the pain and possible injury a fall causes, by removing the rugs. Once you are steady on feet and no longer use any assistive devices, put the rugs back.

Your safety is the most important thing. Under normal circumstances you prevent yourself from falling, by quickly adjusting your feet and body for the stumble. You are unable to make quick adjustments with your feet after surgery.

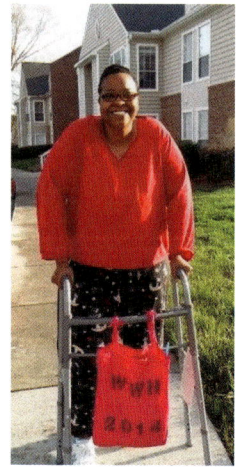

Attaching a bag to the front of the walker makes carrying medication and other supplies easier.

As your knee heals internally and externally at the incision, you experience a variety of sensations. Muscle spasms around the knee are common, side of knee numbness and side of knee burning sensation are also common. As bone, muscle and nerves, heal and regenerate they "talk" to you. Those sensations are your body signal that changes are occurring.

If you had a nerve block (it's highly likely you did), you may also experience pain in the linear area that runs from the groin to the inside of the knee. The nerve numbed during a nerve block runs through this area. It, too, needs to heal. Nerve block pain manifests as a shooting pain or a burning sensation.

Don't panic! These pains are sporadic and do not all occur at once, nor are they continuous. You may feel the sensation for a few minutes at a time, and then it may stop. You experience the periodic sensations until the nerve or muscle generating it heals.

I learned to not complain about all these little aches and pains that come with the surgery. Whenever a new sensation developed, I used it as a sign that my body was healing. I turned the myriad of sensations into a game of sorts. Whenever I experienced a new sensation, I rubbed my knee gently and said, "ohhhh, you're healing, thank you." It sounds ridiculous but it helped me stay positive.

Remember, having a positive attitude about the recovery process makes it easier on you.

Every surgery requires some type of pain reliever. Painkillers do a wonderful job of keeping you comfortable, but they bring an unwanted guest, constipation. Opiate induced constipation is a beast. It makes you doubly miserable. There is nothing worse than the feeling that you gotta go, wanna go, but can't go. It is like sitting on the highway in a traffic jam. You need to get to exit 110 but you are sitting at exit 1. Traffic is not moving at all.

Opiates lock the bowels up. There is no way around that, but there are ways to help get traffic moving again.

Implement a daily routine that includes a stool softener, fiber (fresh fruit, flaxseed, or a fiber mix to add to juice), water (lots and lots of water) and a good probiotic.

Honestly, everything above except the stool softener should be a part of your healthy lifestyle already, right? But if for some reason this is not your regular routine, start it several days before the surgery. I cannot stress enough how important this is. Constipation is no laughing matter!!! Go several days without a bowel movement and you will want to cry.

The above was my routine but I still needed additional help. After being home a few days without a bowel moment, I added a teaspoon of olive oil with lemon juice to the routine each morning before eating anything. The olive oil stimulates the digestive system and gets things moving through your system (plus olive oil is a healthy fat). The lemon juice also stimulates the digestive system and enhances the flavor of the olive oil. You can take either alone, but I wanted something to work, and work quickly.

Following this entire routine (stool softener, fiber, water, a probiotic, and olive oil and lemon juice mix) helped me get back to normal. However, if I missed any part of this regimen, the next day the traffic jam returned.

Keep constipation at bay by implementing a plan and sticking to it. Constipation is an issue while taking prescription pain medication, and continues the entire time you take pain meds.

Two to three weeks after surgery, you have a post-op visit with your surgeon. The surgeon reviews your progress and determines when or if they need to see you again. If your incision had staples and they haven't been removed, they may be removed at this visit. Typically staples are removed around ten days if the incision heals properly. Staples are removed by the home health nurse or physical therapist if your post-op is beyond ten days. If the incision is closed with derma bond (glue used in surgery to bond skin together) there is nothing to remove.

In addition to the external closure, there is an internal closure. Internal stitches are dissoluble so they are not removed. Occasionally an internal stitch works out through the skin before it dissolves completely. This isn't something to worry about. It usually falls off.

By your post-op visit you should be off prescription pain medication, or at least to the point in which it is only needed at night. Talk to your physician, if your need for pain medication has not decreased. Pain killers are addictive. It is a good idea to stop using them as soon as possible!

Record what time you take your pain medication each time you take it. After 2-3 days of taking pills every 4-6 hours 24 hours per day, you will forget what time you took your last dose. Once you stop taking prescription pain meds, record over-the-counter (OTC) medicine intake. Acetaminophen and ibuprofen have guidelines for dosage. Don't take more than the recommended dosage of OTC medicine. It can damage the kidneys and liver.

I used a journal to record my dosage time. I also used it to record how many times I did PT each day, my daily vitamin and supplement and water intake. I created the companion journal to use along with this book for that purpose. (*I Had a Knee Replacement, Now What? 6 Week Companion Journal*).

The incision appears raised after staple removal. It flattens with time. The scar is noticeable, however the skin color slowly returns.

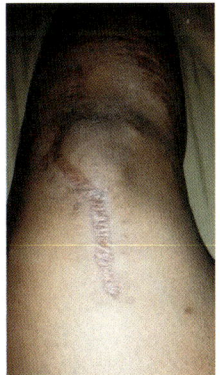

Right leg scar after nine months. The drain location left a slight scar that will eventually fade completely. The scar further on the right is the scar from a previous leg surgery at age 10.

Surgery and recovery take a major toll on the body. The healing process requires a lot of energy. Along with weeks of little activity, the healing process wreaks havoc on stamina. You tire easily and need rest after surgery. The first few weeks seem like an endless cycle of PT and naps. You feel like you need a nap after everything you do. It's all right to nap when you need to, as long as you get your PT in every day. Sleep is restorative and healing. Give your body the rest it needs and the exercise it needs, to rebuild strength and stamina. Stamina increases as you increase your physical activity. It is important to follow your physical therapist guidelines for daily walking. Walking improves your knee function, as well as stamina.

Driving after surgery may occur in as little as 2-3 weeks or as long as 6-7 weeks, depending on which leg it is. Regardless of which leg, be sure to resume driving only after all narcotic pain medication is stopped. Medication impairs judgment and surgery reduces reaction time.

Initially driving is uncomfortable. Your knee aches sitting in the driving position, regardless of which leg it is. Start with short trips around town. Gradually increase the time spent driving. It may take a few months before all driving discomfort leaves.

Expect to feel better every week. Changes occur slowly, but as the weeks pass, expect to feel better, stronger, and more confident.

Ever heard the expression, "Patience is a virtue"? TKR truly puts patience to the test. Boredom and frustration are a part of the process, too!

Pain makes you impatient with yourself and others. The truth is there is no getting around the pain. It is a part of the process. But once you get beyond the pain you have an opportunity for a new life.

During the process, be patient.

Limited mobility causes major boredom, for many. You can't go outside alone, drive, or just get up from a seated position, without what seems like a major theatrical production. Add pain to that mix, and you are on an emotional roller coaster.

You feel happy, sad, mad, glad, frustrated and irritated. Did I mention that this all occurs in an hour? One minute you are happy you had the surgery, then you feel sad because you cannot go outside yet, then mad that you cannot reach that jar in the back of the refrigerator, and overall irritated.

The frustration is the worst. You get excited because you reach 90 degrees flexion today in PT but then wake up the next day at 85 degrees flexion again. This happens over and over.

Be patient with yourself. Recovery is a long process. Over the coming weeks the stiffness in the morning decreases. In the beginning it is a daily occurrence.

Be patient. Listen to music or a book. You will likely tire of television pretty quickly. Have other activities to engage in that you enjoy. I ordered an adult coloring book online, and spent many afternoons coloring. It was fun and it eased the feelings of frustration and boredom.

It is not uncommon to experience some anxiety or fear about what to expect after surgery.

Try this simple exercise to release your anxiety now and throughout your healing journey.

Close your eyes and take a slow, deep breathe Slowly count to 5. Slowly release the breathe until the lungs are completely empty. Repeat the slow deep breathe three times. Open your eyes.

How do you feel now?

_____

_____

_____

_____

Deep breathing calms the central nervous system. Deep breathing creates clarity and deep breathing also reduces pain. Use this technique throughout the healing journey to reduce anxiety, frustration and pain.

Remember three things:

1. This is temporary.

2. The long-term reward far exceeds the short-term discomfort associated with recovery.

3. You WIN!

Say aloud:

I Win!

I WIN!!

I WIN!!!!

CHAPTER THREE
PHYSICAL THERAPY

Not every pain comes to harm you.
- Sicilian Proverb

Physical therapy (PT) is defined as:

the treatment of disease, injury, or disability by physical and mechanical means (such as massage, regulated exercise, water, light, heat, and electricity).

After TKR, PT is designed to increase the range of motion, strength and flexibility.

There is a quote by Benjamin Franklin that states, "Those things that hurt, instruct." That quote essentially means that challenges make you stronger. Benjamin Franklin probably wasn't thinking about PT when he said it, but it definitely makes me think about PT.

In the case of PT, those things that hurt, build. PT is challenging but it definitely makes you stronger. PT increases flexion (the extent to which your knee bends) and extension (how flat your knee lies with a straight leg), builds muscle and increases stamina and endurance. In addition, PT builds your confidence.

PT is an integral part of recovery from orthopedic surgery. This is especially true after TKR. Don't do the PT, you don't regain function.

After most surgeries the patient spends the day in bed. The day of total knee replacement the physical therapist comes not to visit, but to put you to work. However, don't panic. That first visit isn't too traumatic. Typically during the first session, the therapist has you sit on the side of the bed and possibility stand up. It benefits you greatly to get up and moving. Getting out of bed increases blood circulation and reduces the risk of blood clots.

The therapist may have you perform a few simple exercises to see how far your knee bends. This will hurt a bit, but it is not excruciatingly painful. Move slowly and carefully to avoid a sudden jolt of pain, and your first session will go smoothly.

For many patients that first PT session evokes fear. There is the fear of pain, the fear of falling while standing on a newly operated knee, and uncertainty in their ability to walk on an artificial knee. While these fears are justifiable, don't let them terrorize you. The therapist is there to keep you safe and show you how to do things properly, so you don't fall or otherwise hurt yourself. If they need additional assistance, they always have an aid or nurse close by to assist you.

The therapist visits you daily while hospitalized. The goal at this stage of PT is for you to walk down the hall with the use of the walker. If a patient has difficulty bending the knee, the physician may order a continuous passive motion (CPM) machine to use once released from the hospital. However, the overall effectiveness of CPMs is still being investigated. As such, many health insurance companies don't cover it, or require special medical requirements to be met.

Home PT starts once you are discharged from the hospital. The first in home PT session should be within 1-2 days of discharge. In-home PT usually last 2-3 weeks. The therapist visits 2-3 times per week for 1 hour sessions. With each session, the therapist adds additional exercises to your regimen.

There are a variety of exercises. Each exercise works to increase range of motion, strength and flexibility. The exercises change and increase in difficulty as you progress and get stronger.

Your post-operative visit typically occurs just as home PT is about to end. Based on your progress your orthopedist may refer you to outpatient PT. If your range of motion (flexion and extension) is good, outpatient PT may not be required.

I definitely needed outpatient PT for my right knee. After my incision revision surgery, in-home PT stopped for ten days. My knee was immobilized in a straight leg brace. My knee was extremely stiff after the stitches and brace were removed. However, my progress with the left knee was great. At my post-op visit, I had well over 100 degrees of flexion (knee bend) and 0 degrees extension (leg laid flat) so my surgeon stated that I didn't necessarily need it. I chose to go to outpatient PT because years of arthritis in both knees left me weak. I went to develop more strength, balance and flexibility.

Outpatient PT also lasts for 1 hour. It begins with a 5 minute warm-up on an exercise bike or seated elliptical. The warm-up is followed by individually performed exercises such as leg lifts, heel slides and a variety of other exercises. The individually performed exercises are followed by manual manipulation. The session ends with 10 minutes of icing the joint.

Manual manipulation involves the therapist manually assisting you perform certain movements to encourage the joint to bend more.

That bend is measured in degrees. 90 degrees is considered to be a functioning knee. However, many daily activities such as getting in a bath tub or squatting require much more flexion. The more flexion or bend you regain, the more activities you can engage in.

It is not uncommon to experience some degree of pain during physical therapy. An important distinction to make during PT is the distinction between discomfort and actual pain.

Discomfort is the lack of physical comfort.

Pain is the physical feeling caused by disease, injury or something that hurts the body.

Your body went through major trauma and is still healing. The incision, muscles and bones are all healing. Most everything is uncomfortable and causes discomfort at this stage. Physical therapy, sleeping and performing daily tasks cause discomfort, but is it actually painful?

Sometimes it is and sometimes it isn't. That is a distinction you need to make. Sometimes PT is painful but other times it is uncomfortable. Knowing the difference helps you push your way through the discomfort.

When you experience discomfort during manual manipulation, allow the therapist to continue to work. It's that little extra push just past discomfort that reaps major gains in flexion. Every degree of range of motion you regain increases your ability to perform everyday tasks. Telling the therapist to stop during the discomfort phase only slows down your progress and increases the length of time you need PT.

The expression, "time is money," is true. Every time you step through the door for PT requires money for the service. The longer you require PT, the more money it costs you.

Once you reach the point in which there is an increase in pain, it is all right to say that's enough.

The best technique to use that allows you to better tolerate discomfort and pain, is deep breathing.

Take slow, long, deep breathes. When the therapist needs to hold a position for 5-10 seconds, continue to practice deep breathing through it. Holding your breath increases pain. Unfortunately, the first thing most people do when they experience pain is hold their breathe.

Everyone has a different pain threshold. Some people have a high pain threshold while others have a very low one. That's okay.

Don't measure yourself against others, just do your absolute best.

Most PT rooms are common areas in which several patients are present. People are different ages and physical conditions, with different injuries or surgeries. Don't measure yourself by what someone else in the room does. They have a different story even if you had the same surgery. Therefore, do YOUR best. If you know you did your personal best, that is all you can ask of yourself.

The simple formula for PT is

PATIENCE + PASSION + PERSISTENCE = SUCCESS

Be patient with yourself and your progress. Work hard every day and do YOUR best. Let your best be enough because it is enough. Throughout recovery your best looks different, based on many factors. You can't ask any more of yourself than your best. Celebrate each success, every degree gained, and every new milestone reached.

Be passionate about your PT. Being passionate means you are emotionally and physically vested in your success. Don't give up. If you can't get past 95 degrees or whatever that magic number is for you this week, be persistent. Keep trying, you'll get there. You will achieve your goals.

Persistence means you consistently do your PT. Consistently doing PT means you do PT EVERYDAY whether you feel like it or not! You don't cancel PT appointments unless there is a legitimate reason to do so. Just so you know, "I don't feel like PT today" is not a legitimate reason to cancel an at-home session or outpatient session. If you feel badly enough to cancel a session, than you should call your doctor and inform them of any symptoms you experience. On a day-to-day basis you should feel better, not worse.

On a scale of 1 to 10 (where 1 is not at all and 10 is extremely), how passionate are you about your recovery? _____

What can you do to be more passionate about your recovery?

_____

_____

_____

_____

_____

Besides experiencing less pain, why did you get your knee(s) replaced (to play with kids or grandkids, travel, hike, etc.)?

_____

_____

_____

_____

_____

That's your motivation! Use your goals, dreams and hope for your future to motivate, inspire and propel you forward.

CHAPTER FOUR
RECONNECT

Look to the past to help us move forward in the future.
- Ghanaian Proverb

In today's day and age, we are perpetually in a state of constant disconnect. We are tuned into electronics/technology more than ever and are living a fast-paced/plugged-in existence. We work more hours than ever before, we sleep less, are less active, and are the unhealthiest we've ever been. We are losing ourselves in the process. We disconnect from ourselves when we experience pain in our lives and within our bodies, we disconnect from our breath during times of stress and anxiety, we disconnect from ourselves when we become overwhelmed. With each time we disconnect with our inner self, we create tension within our body.

Tension and "stuckness" in the body are like a contracted and tight fist. With each tense reaction, the body adds to this contraction making the overall tension increase, tightening the tissues, muscles, and joints restricting movement and breath. This chronic tension/contraction leads further into the disassociation of self. With every moment of connectedness and relaxation, the contraction comes undone a bit calming the body of this chronic tension and helping heal you of your pain.

Exercise: Practice becoming aware of the tension within your body. Begin first by clenching and relaxing your jaw. Move next to shrugging and relaxing your shoulders. Moving down, clench and relax your hands, really focusing on increasing the tension within your fists and arms, then really relaxing it all out. Notice what it is to be tense and then become aware of the sensations of relaxation. Practice with other muscle groups to create a greater awareness of yourself and your body.

Reconnecting to the Physical Body

By now, you may be nearing the end of your current healing journey or just beginning one. It isn't always necessarily going to be a pleasant journey. You experience the pains from surgery, physical therapy, and every day soreness. It is during this time period that you begin to disassociate from yourself, specifically the area you are experiencing pain, whether it be from a trauma or surgery.

In today's society, we tend to look at PAIN as an annoyance or nuisance that is disturbing our life, but, what if your pain is trying to tell you something? What if your pain was trying to tell you to "Stop" what you're doing, by purposefully interrupting your life in order for you to make a change?

The time is now, to love the parts of you that are ailing. Your knee/hip/foot/back, is not a separate entity, it is a part of you. Especially during the healing process you must love ALL of your parts, even if you find it physically uncomfortable. During this time of pain, discomfort, and disassociation, you may begin making statements such as "My knee is killing me!" Instead, change that question and ask yourself "Why am I killing my knee?" Changing how you view pain will begin your personal transformation with reconnecting back to your body. This part of you is not going anywhere and the longer you recognize it as something separate, the longer your healing journey will be. Utilize this discomfort that you might be experiencing as FUEL for growth, because once this journey is over, it's time to start a new chapter in your life.

Reconnecting back to a part of yourself can be as easy as placing your hand on your painful areas and breathing deeply allowing your breath to flow into that area. It's almost as if you are saying "Hello" and acknowledging this part of you. Your breathing should be in through your nose and out through your mouth focusing your breath, energy, and awareness into this specific area.

It is when you begin to reconnect to your body, you regain the sense to understand your rhythms and how you heal. When you are capable to breathe through your entire spine and your nervous system is free of interference, you are able to understand the subtle cues that your body gives you. Your body is amazing. Your body has the innate capacity to heal itself. You are intelligently designed to move freely, breathe deeply, and to thrive!

Our bodies are magnificent creations, and with the right resources and guidance healing will occur. When you begin paying attention to the subtleties of yourself, your body will give way to the tensions, shallow/constricted breathing, and lack or loss of movement, and begin to open to the endless potential of full health and well-being. When you begin to reconnect with your body and your rhythms, you may find it difficult at first. You have to unlearn the years of "interruptions," the scars of surgery, the doubt and limiting beliefs of the mind, the restricted movement, and the postural compensations. With guidance, time, and practice, you will be back in tune with your inner self.

"Re-membering is literally the process of putting back together again the fractured and scattered pieces that have come apart. Integrating body, mind, and breath through the practice of breathing and self-love/care helps us remember."[1]

Reconnecting to the Body via Breath

When we are born, we are instinctively aware of our inner self cues; our hunger, tiredness, and our genuine sense of comfort & discomfort. We are instinctively wired to listen to our inner cues for survival. We begin our life journey with it, and we end our human experience with it; it's the first to escape us when we are excited or frightened…We Breathe…Our breath is what sets the TONE of our consciousness. It is the language of our soul, the song of our spine, the rhythm that releases the past and the present tension into a more peaceful now. We disconnect when we feel overwhelmed and we breathe more fully when we are safe and relaxed. As a result of stress, our breath becomes labored and shallow.

Unfortunately, as we grow, stress, disconnect and disassociate with ourselves, we begin to limit ourselves and restrict and/or hold our breath. We have slowly stopped listening to our internal cues and begun focusing more on our external environment for cues. We have slowly disconnected from our inner innate wisdom and rhythms, for an external, educated, thinking form. We begin to externally follow popular culture for cues on what is defined as normal. We no longer know when to eat, sleep, or move, without a device or external contraption. Thus, we are the most obese, unhealthy, sleep deprived, disconnected country. We need to go through an unlearning process in order to experience the fullness of ourselves and our lives. Conscious breathing has been said to be the number one healing practice because your breath plays a major role in your health, consciousness, healing, and well-being.

With each breath, it is an opportunity to enjoy being ALIVE, and it doesn't cost a thing. You already have unlimited access to this unlimited supply of your breath, you just have to tap into it by becoming more aware. With each inhalation, you are receiving sustenance, and with each exhalation, you are releasing that which no longer serves you.

Your breath is one of the most underutilized healing mechanisms used today and it is also one of the most powerful. Breathing is always accessible to us; we [1]can utilize it while we're at work, home, or a restaurant. We have this amazing self-healing tool already built inside of us. Not only is breath important for getting oxygen to the rest of our body, it also creates movement to all of our vital organs

---

[1] Johnson, Will. Breathing Through The Whole Body. Rochester, Vt.: Inner Traditions, 2012. Print.

in our body. From massaging our stomach, intestines, and liver, to

creating movement in the most important organ system in our body, the spine and nervous system.

Reconnecting with the Body through Movement

We are designed to move.

Physical exercise and movement is essential to our existence. We evolved as humans while living an active creative lifestyle and we function best when we remain active and fit. Our blood is constantly flowing, our heart pumping, our lungs expanding/contracting, our nerve fibers sending signals, and our cells constantly vibrating. We are moving with life's expression.

After experiencing trauma, it is sometimes difficult to move. You have to re-learn certain movements after a traumatic surgery. Difficulty moving and being active after trauma and surgery is normal. Your body needs time to heal after traumatic experiences, hence inflammation, stiffness, and achiness. Unfortunately during the healing process, you may experience pain, varying setbacks, and complications, which is all a part of each individual healing journey. Learn to listen to the subtle cues of your body as you learn to move while healing.

Just as in physical therapy, you have to customize everything in your life to fit and accommodate this new and healing you. Listen to the subtleties and the cues your body is giving you to thrive. Drink more water, eat better, limit processed foods during these critical healing months, use warm/cold compresses for circulation, move and getting active in new ways that won't cause injury to your healing tissue/cells/body, stretch, meditate, laugh, cry, pray, sing, talk with loved ones, LISTEN.

Make a list of at least 5 activities/hobbies that you enjoy and dedicate some time each day/week to doing at least one off your list. Keep this list of 5 in front of you so you can see it every day!

1._____

2._____

3._____

4._____

5._____

Now make a list of 5 activities that you've always wanted to try or haven't been able to do since your injury/trauma/surgery. This list will be a reminder for what's to come once your healing is further along. Keep these 5 to encourage you.

1._____

2._____

3._____

4._____

5._____

Reconnecting via Chiropractic

Our nervous system is the most important organ system in our body. It consists of our brain, spinal cord, and the nerves that run throughout our entire body. The nervous system job is to make sure we walk, talk, digest food, see, smell, hear, heal, the list goes on and on. When the brain is able to communicate with the rest of the body through the spinal cord without interference, your body is capable of healing itself. Doctors of Chiropractic are specialists of the nervous system and are capable locating areas of interference within your spinal cord. Many times people think that Chiropractors only focus on getting people out of pain, however, that is quite the contrary. Chiropractors focus on removing the interference from your nervous system so that your body is capable of utilizing its innate abilities to heal itself and rid itself from pain.

The brain and body are interconnected: the brain thinks and the body feels. The brain sends messages and the body responds, and vice versa. This integration of these two interconnected systems communicates via the spinal cord (nerve fibers) and nervous system. The nervous system is comprised of the brain, spinal column, and the spinal nerves. Flowing from the brain in the spinal cord, is nerve tissue. This tissue (nerve fibers) run throughout the spines central canal (the spinal column containing 24 flexible bones). This boney column is for protection of this very delicate and vitally important nervous tissue. Between each of the 24 flexible bones, the nerves branch, much like that of branches of a tree, in order to control and coordinate ALL of our actions and reactions.

Sometimes our breath gets trapped/stuck/restricted and is unable to flow freely beyond this wall of tension, the stuck joint, or the area of pain and lack of motion. With the guidance of a skilled chiropractor, they will be able to assist your body in letting go of that stored (stuck) tension/pain/disconnection thus allowing your breath to once again move freely throughout your entire body. We remove blocks within your nervous system, and bring awareness of the unconscious defense and tension patterns held within your body by mobilizing the "stuck" joints/tissues in order to increase neuronal firing (messages from the brain to the body and body to brain) and inner awareness back into your body. You are then able to move more unrestricted, connect with those parts that were "stuck" and energetically disconnected, and breath more freely and fully throughout your whole entire body!

Breath is just the means. Movement is just the means. Chiropractic is just the means. The real goal of this practice is to fully experience and become more aware of what happens to you- your mind, your body, your sense of self, your understanding of your incarnation, your healing journey- when you explore and reconnect with your entire body. Who do you become once you are connected? How different would your life be if yourself, your breath, your body had permission to feel and heal?

It takes very serious and continually renewed commitment to live, love, eat, move, breathe, and express fully and consciously … Staying mindful on this journey will require active participation and continuous commitment, however, you will find yourself living a more connected and full life.

It's your time to THRIVE. Live connected.

CHAPTER FOUR RECONNECT written by contributing authors.

~Dr. Krishana Clark and Dr. Chris Girdis of TLC: The Lifestyle Center~

CHAPTER FIVE
GOALS

Keep your eye upon the goal.
- Latin Proverb

There is no question about it, recovery from total knee replacement is challenging. However, take comfort in the fact that you made the best decision for you based on your needs.

To achieve the best long-term results, make choices that support your long-term goals.

Goals are important in every aspect of life. Goals provide a vision for the future. That vision provides motivation to achieve short-term goals. Reaching short-term goals motivates you to achieve long-term goals.

After TKR, one of the first goals your surgeon and physical therapist sets is to reach 90 degrees. It is important that you establish additional goals for yourself throughout your recovery. The simple act of setting those goals will motivate and inspire you.

Begin with short-term goals you can achieve within a week or two. As you gain strength and function, set a slightly bigger goal. A slightly bigger goal is one that requires hard work, yet is still achievable.

Set your first goal after your first in-home PT session. You need to know your starting point before you set your goals. Set a new goal for the next week. The physical therapist sets goals for you, but it a good idea to set goals for yourself that compliment your PT goals. Examples include:

1. Put on your socks and shoes.

2. Walk to the mailbox (once cleared to go outside).

3. Walk down the block.

4. Start walking with a cane.

5. Walk around the block.

6. Walk without a cane.

Your initial goals may be more challenging. The idea is to set goals that work for you.

The goals should be progressive yet achievable. Goals are different for everyone based on your functionality and progress, so establish goals that fit your level of ability.

After my left knee replacement, I was able to put on my socks and shoes immediately. I was not able to put on my socks and shoes immediately after my right knee replacement. My right knee was severely damaged and the surgery took longer. As a result there was more soft tissue damage. There was more pain and swelling. However, I was able to put on my socks and shoes within a few days.

The short-term goal for my right knee was 90 degrees as with any TKR. But the long-term goal for it was only 95 degrees, due to the fact that it didn't bend to 90 degrees prior to surgery. But I was determined to gain more functionality. I set a goal of 100 degrees for myself. I wanted to regain as much function as possible. By the time PT ended for my right knee I was at 102 degrees.

I realized I was capable of doing more, so I vowed to continue PT even though my sessions were over. Over the next five months, I did PT exercises on my own. When I had my left knee done, I had the same physical therapist, so he measured my right knee as well. I was at 106 degrees. So I set another goal of 110 degrees.

Every time I did PT for my left knee, I did PT for my right knee. When I completed PT for my left knee, my right knee flexion was

115 degrees. That is a whopping 20 degrees more than what was ever expected!

Every degree gained increases your ability to perform everyday tasks. 90 degrees is a functioning knee. You can stand, sit, walk, and climb stairs with a 90 degree knee, but a normal knee bends to about 130-135 degrees (120 degrees is about the most seen in TKR recipients). Every additional degree increases your ability to perform other tasks.

To get what you want in life, you have to know what you want. What do you want for yourself?

Week 1 goal. _____

_____

_____

_____

_____

Week 2 goal. _____

_____

_____

_____

_____

Week 3 goal. _____

_____

_____

_____

_____

Week 4 goal. _____

_____

_____

_____

_____

Set a new goal with every new milestone reached. Establishing new goals keep you excited about your progress.

In addition to short-term goals, you need long-term goals as well.

Long-term goals are just what the name implies. They are goals that take longer to achieve. Long-term goals with your career usually are one, five or maybe even 10 years. Recovery long-term goals differ in that it typically is a shorter time period. Big changes occur in less time.

3 month goal. _____

_____

_____

_____

_____

6 month goal. _____

_____

_____

_____

_____

I had one long-term goal, to hike. Yes, I wanted to be in less pain but more than anything I wanted to regain my mobility so I could spend time in nature. So my goals revolved around walking, such as walk one mile, walk two miles on treadmill, walk a natural trail, walk around a lake and so forth.

I am an outdoor person. I was always an outdoor person. I spent the last 10 years indoors. Now I spend every minute I can outdoors. My greatest desire is to spend hours wondering through the woods. As such, my long-term goal is to hike natural trails in all

50 states, not hike 50 states, which implies walking across the U.S.!

Thanks to getting both knees replaced, that goal is achievable. To prepare for hiking many miles, I go camping and hiking with my family. I am loving every minute of my new life. I am loving every minute of my new-found freedom.

That one goal alone was enough to motivate me on my most tired and frustrated days.

What is your long-term goal (12 months or longer)? (Hint: use your motivation established in the PT chapter to set your long-term goal).

_____

_____

_____

_____

_____

Kimberly Dixon, M.Ed., CPC, CCRC

CONCLUSION

I wish no one had to go through the aftermath of surgery. I wish you had your surgery and viola, everything is normal, healed and functioning properly. Unfortunately, that is not how the body works. It requires time to heal and recover after trauma.

Knowing what to expect after TKR serves several purposes:

1. It eases anxiety about the surgery. Our imagination is a beautiful gift, but let it run wild, and it has the capability to completely terrorize us. Knowing what to expect prevents the imagination from keeping you awake at night before the surgery.

2. It helps you prepare before the surgery actually occurs. Knowing what to expect prepares you mentally and physically for what is about to occur.

3. It lets you know that you are not alone. Everyone experiences some degree of pain after TKR and everyone experiences frustration. What you experience after is normal for most people.

Physical therapy is a big part of recovery after TKR. Your commitment to PT sets the tone for your recovery. Remember,

PATIENCE + PASSION + PERSISTENCE = SUCCESS

Be patient. Be passionate. Be persistent.

You are worth it!

After TKR take the time to reconnect to your life. Reconnect with family and friends and other parts of your social circle. You may not notice the changes you make to your life because of pain because they are gradual. Many chronic pain suffers withdraw from life. They stop engaging in activities they enjoy because of pain or the fear of increased pain.

Reconnect to your life.

It is imperative to also reconnect to your body. You naturally compensate for pain. That compensation is unnatural and puts strain on your entire body. Over time, these unnatural movements have a negative impact on your back, hips, neck and shoulders.

I had arthritis for 33 years. The last 10 years I used my arms to assist in standing. The small muscles in my back, shoulders and neck were not designed to do the work of large thigh muscles. My spine is misaligned and I literally have knots of tight muscles (trigger points) all over my body.

In addition, I was born with bow-legs. My right leg was more bowed than the left which means my hips never sat evenly. TKR corrected that misalignment. My hips sat evenly for the first time ever and my body knew it. My muscular hip pain after knee surgery was intense. My muscles were so tight. Tight muscles hurt, a lot!

To reconnect to my physical body I resumed adaptive yoga classes. (I started adaptive yoga three years ago as part of my arthritis pain management regimen). In addition I sought out a chiropractor that uses a more gentle approach than the traditional cracking and popping of traditional chiropractic care and I sought out a medical masseuse. (A medical masseuse does deep tissue massage that releases trigger points).

Thanks to adaptive yoga, spinal adjustments and trigger point release my body released the tension patterns held for years. I am now pain free for the first in decades.

Don't skip this step.

Reconnecting to your body is important. Every part of your body is connected to another part. Retrain the body to function properly.

Your body may not require as much as mine did, but you owe it to yourself to give your body what it needs.

Your entire recovery is surrounded by goals. Set goals throughout the process to motivate, inspire and set yourself up for success.

You can do this! Recovery is just part of the process. What's on the other side of recovery is an opportunity for a beautiful life.

Every week there is less pain and discomfort. Every week there is more mobility and function. Every week you feel better physically, spiritually and mentally.

Don't give up. Always remember, YOU WIN!

Again, congratulations on your knee replacement(s).

Welcome to our exclusive club and welcome to your new life!

Kimberly Dixon, M.Ed., CPC, CCRC

SOURCES

"World English Bible" and worldenglishbible.org are trademarks. Permission is granted to use the name "World English Bible" and its logo only to identify faithful copies of the public domain translation of the Holy Bible of that name published at ebible.org and worldenglishbible.org. The World English Bible is not copyrighted.

Ancient Proverbs:
http://www.worldofproverbs.com/2012/05/public-domain-published-before-1923.html

Inspirational Proverbs:
http://www.inspirationalstories.com/proverbs/

Cover Image: Knee X Ray

Credit line © Sphotography | Dreamstime.com

Cover Design: Lindagraphix

Image: Knee Joint Labeled Diagram

Credit line © Rob3000 | Dreamstime.com

Image: Knee with prosthesis

Credit line © Stefano Panzeri | Dreamstime.com

Image: Stages of knee Osteoarthritis (OA)

Credit Line © Designua | Dreamstime.com

Image: Total knee replacement surgery

Credit Line © Alila07 | Dreamstime.com

Physical therapy, discomfort and pain definition taken from
www.merriam-webster.com

ADDITIONAL RESOURCES

Blog on arthritis and mental, physical and spiritual well-being: www.bowlegsandarthritis.com

See videos of my hospital stay and recovery process. YouTube channel, Joyful Living: https://www.youtube.com/channel/UCRiB9_be_VmI1s20CoZqZAg

Looking for a life coach to help your deal with chronic pain? Visit www.joyfullivingwithkimberlydixon.com

Look for more books in the Now What? series:

I Have Arthritis, Now What? (Ways To Manage Arthritis Pain)

I Need a Knee Replacement, Now What? (How To Prepare for Knee Replacement Surgery)

I Had a Knee Replacement, Now What? (Six Week Companion Journal)

Kimberly Dixon, M.Ed., CPC, CCRC

REVIEWS

This is a great resource to learn exactly what to expect after surgery. I wish this was available to me prior to having knee replacement surgery. It helps to have the author's personal experience and to brace yourself for those up and downs days. This is a great resource to share with anyone considering the pros and cons of knee replacement.

Thena A. (knee replacement recipient) Raleigh, NC

I Had a Knee Replacement, Now What?, flows smoothly with knowledge and personality. The simplicity of the message encourages the reader to take authority over the process of recovering from joint replacement, healing and wholeness. In a place once garnered by limited mobility, the book grants one the power to join life with a new sense of stability and possibly.

Valerie D. (hip replacement recipient) Belews Creek, NC

This is a comprehensive and accessible guide for anyone facing knee surgery. The author offers first hand perspective on the important truths of the before, during and after of knee replacement surgery. She offers innumerable useful insights that assist in understanding every aspect of the process, allowing the reader to achieve the best possible outcome from his/her journey.

Saisha R. Madrid, Spain

Kim addresses the issues to achieve a healthy surgical result that many people tend to overlook or minimize. They are very similar to what my struggles and successes were with hip replacement surgery. I encourage any surgical candidate to explore this perspective.

Dr. Howie Shareff, RYT

ABOUT THE CONTRIBUTING AUTHORS

Krishana Clark, B.S., C-PT, D.C was always interested in the intricate workings of the human body. From the way we move to the way we heal, our bodies provide us with the capacity to experience the world.

After a bachelor's degree in kinesiology from Michigan State University, she became a personal trainer for several years helping people achieve their personal wellness goals through fitness and re-educating the body and its movement patterns. She didn't feel complete in stopping there, so she decided to further her education at Life University in Marietta, GA in order to become a chiropractor. Chiropractic care gave Dr. Clark a way to safely enhance a person's quality of life without the use of drugs or surgeries.

Dr. Clark chose Network Chiropractic because she believes it is the most effective way to help people heal from the everyday traumas, toxins, and thoughts that lead to stress or tension in your system, and to integrate these aspects for a greater expression of one's self.

Christopher Girdis, B.S, D.C. received his Bachelors of Science degree from University of Massachusetts-Dartmouth in Business Marketing while playing football for all four years. Upon graduation, he started a career in sales and marketing. He came to the realization that there is more to this life than trying to make people money. He knew that he wanted to help others and was fortunate to find chiropractic care, where he was given the opportunity to help people reconnect with themselves and which allows Dr. Girdis to make a positive impact on the world we live in.

He attended Life University, where he obtained a Doctor of Chiropractic degree. During his time at Life he found Network Spinal Analysis, which gave him a gift that keeps on giving. This work had a big impact on his life physically, emotionally, and spiritually. While at the University he held a leadership role in Network Spinal Analysis Club on Campus and also obtained a Level 1 and 2 certification in Network Care. Dr. Girdis is extremely excited to serve the people of The Triangle (Raleigh-Durham-Chapel Hill NC) and the surrounding community.

ABOUT THE AUTHOR

Kimberly Dixon, M.Ed., CPC, CRCC holds a Master's degree in education with her focus on psychology. She is a certified professional coach, a certified Christian coach and a neuro-linguistic programming practitioner. In addition, she is a blogger and speaker.

In her life, she had eight surgeries on her legs and knees (after three surgeries in 2015, the surgery count is at eleven). Each surgery was different from the other in regards to recovery time, physical therapy, and pain level. The one thing they all had in common was that they taught her something different. The daily struggles, surgeries and pain endured taught her many valuable lessons about life, health, happiness and perseverance. The purpose of the *Now What* series and blog is to share her experiences with others and perhaps helps someone else experiencing a similar situation. Her coaching practice, specializes in coaching people with chronic pain or chronic illnesses.

59010197R00045

Made in the USA
Charleston, SC
25 July 2016